How Things Are Made

Trees to Paper

By Inez Snyder

Welcome Books™

SCHOLASTIC INC.
New York Toronto London Auckland Sydney
Mexico City New Delhi Hong Kong Buenos Aires

Flansburg

Photo Credits: Cover © Premium Stock/Corbis; p. 5, 21 (upper left) © Stuart Westmorland/ Corbis; p. 7 © Kevin Fleming/Corbis; p. 9, 21 (upper right) © David Lees/Corbis; p. 11 © Morton Beebe/Corbis; p. 13, 15, 17, 21(lower left and lower right) © Ecoscene/Corbis; p. 19 © Nancy Sheehan/Index Stock Imagery, Inc.
Contributing Editor: Jennifer Silate
Book Design: Mindy Liu

ISBN 0-516-24453-1

12 11 10 9 8 7 6 5 4 3   3 4 5 6 7 8/0

Printed in the U.S.A.   61

First Scholastic club printing, October 2003

Contents

Paper is made from trees.

The wood from the trees is cut into small **pieces**.

Water and **chemicals** are added to the wood.

This **mixture** is called **pulp**.

The pulp is put
into **machines**.

The pulp is wet.

11

Then, the pulp is **spread** out flat on a machine.

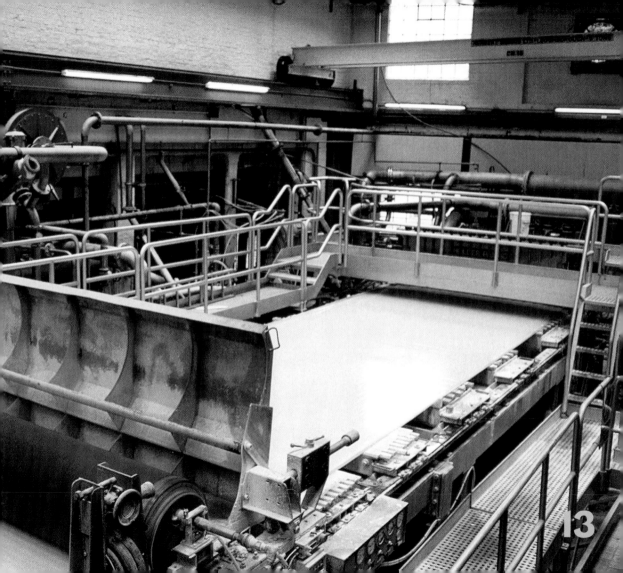

13

The pulp goes through many machines.

This machine dries the pulp.

The dry pulp is paper.

15

This machine cuts the paper into different sizes.

Paper is used for many things.

We write and draw on paper.

Many things must be done to make paper from trees.

New Words

chemicals (**kem**-uh-kuhlz) substances used
in chemistry
machines (muh-**sheenz**) equipment with moving
parts that are used to do a job
mixture (**miks**-chur) something that is made up of
different things mixed together
pieces (**peess**-uhz) bits of something larger
pulp (**puhlp**) a soft, wet mixture of wood
and chemicals
spread (**spred**) to unfold or stretch out

To Find Out More

Books
Paper
by Annabelle Dixon
Garrett Educational

Papermaking for Kids
by Beth Wilkinson
Gibbs Smith, Publisher

Web Site
Paper University
http://www.tappi.org/paperu
Play fun games and learn about paper and how it is made
on this Web site.

Index

About the Author

Inez Snyder writes and edits children's books. She also enjoys painting and cooking for her family.

Reading Consultants

Kris Flynn, Coordinator, Small School District Literacy, The San Diego County Office of Education

Shelly Forys, Certified Reading Recovery Specialist, W.J. Zahnow Elementary School, Waterloo, IL

Sue McAdams, Former President of the North Texas Reading Council of the IRA, and Early Literacy Consultant, Dallas, TX